VER

VERSES

Margaret Planner

ARTHUR H. STOCKWELL LTD.
Torrs Park Ilfracombe Devon
Established 1898
www.ahstockwell.co.uk

First published in Great Britain, 2006

British Library Cataloguing-in-Publication Data.
A catalogue record for this book is available from the British Library.

ISBN 0-7223-3772-8
ISBN 978-0-7223-3772-1
Printed in Great Britain by
Arthur H. Stockwell Ltd.
Torrs Park Ilfracombe
Devon

Contents

The Men in My Life	7
Easter	8
Matins	9
Love Letter	10
On the Prayer List	11
Timothy 3, Mary Jane 0	12
The Vandals	13
Bereavement	14
The Old Tub's Prayer	15
The Flower Festival	16
M. A. P. - OAP	17
The Blind Man	18
St Giles	20
St Giles the Abbot	21
Mrs McCarthy	22
The Convalescent Home	23
Spring	24
Father Knows Best	25
Thoughts of a Senior Citizen	26
Words from Chambers Dictionary	27
McTavish	28
The Skies	29
England	30
Christmas	31
At Your Service	32
Nil Desperandum!	33
NHS	34
The Pearly Gates	35
Love Letters	36
Road Rage	37
The Queen's English	38
Medical History	39
Strained Relations	40

The Men in My Life

As I am growing older now
I sometimes wonder why
I didn't seek a husband
Who was good at DIY.
However, I can't say
I'm not contented with my lot,
As really I'm quite happy
With the helpers I have got.
There is Bill who brings the milk round,
And Peter brings the mail;
There's Tom who tends the garden,
And they're never known to fail.
There's Harry who's electric,
And there's Charlie who is gas -
They will always give assistance
To a semi-senile lass.
Then John collects the laundry,
And young William clears the drains,
While Michael cleans the windows,
Unless of course it rains.
It's Robert who's the plumber,
And Graham mends the car,
And Terry drives a taxi
If I'm going very far.
Patrick does the painting,
And young Richard gives advice -
Of course I never take it,
But the thoughtfulness is nice.
I have to pay the bills,
But then how really good it feels
To get this kind assistance
And not have to cook their meals.

Easter

Easter is a time for chocolate
Eggs and hot cross buns.
For holidays from work and school
And seeking foreign suns.
And just like the millennium
There are some people who,
When asked what it's about,
Just simply haven't got a clue.
But still the Christians celebrate
Their age-old faith and hope,
And pray, with charity,
The others find that they can cope.

Matins

The matins congregation is,
On the whole, mature,
And some of us have aches and pains
The doctors cannot cure.
Most of us have heartaches
For the loved ones who have gone,
And some have come to find the strength
That helps them carry on.
We all have happy memories –
In fact, a goodly store.
There's not much you can tell us
That we haven't heard before.
When sunshine lights the windows,
They are beautiful to see,
And those who know they can get up
Get down on bended knee.
We're hardly ever riotous,
But quietly in the pew
We worship as our forbears did
In 1662.
The rector leads the service –
We follow as we ought.
He looks affectionately down
And gives us food for thought.
Oh, what a joy on Sundays,
At a quarter past eleven,
To rest awhile, and ponder
On the rocky road to Heaven!

Love Letter

I love you, he wrote, with all of my heart.
My life is empty when we're apart.
I'd climb a mountain to be with you,
I'd swim the seas if you asked me to.
My love will never ever grow less,
Your smile means everything, dear. PS:
The weather forecast is most unsound -
If it rains tomorrow, I won't be round.

On the Prayer List

I believe in prayer – I have reason to.
At my lowest ebb it has helped me through.
It has helped me rise when I thought I'd fall,
Though it wasn't the prayers *I* prayed at all,
But the prayers of my friends, and my loved ones too,
And of unknown Christians, like you and you.

Timothy 3, Mary Jane 0

Mary Jane was left in the lurch
Before she had even arrived at the church.
She was all in white when the message came:
'I'm off to a special football game.
Let's make it Thursday at half past two.'
And he signed it, 'Timothy - I love you.'
On Thursday a messenger on his bike
Arrived with a letter: 'If you like,
I could make it Friday, but not today;
I've just discovered they're playing away.'
Friday dawned, and the blushing bride
Was informed by postcard, 'My love, my side
Is through to the final this afternoon,
But with any luck I'll be with you soon.'
Mary Jane was simple, but not that thick -
She went round to give him a penalty kick.
Although she knew he was quite a good catch,
It didn't look like a benefit match.

The Vandals

The vandals have been in the churchyard again;
They've damaged the stone that is over Aunt Jane.
If she were alive, she would give them what for;
But in any event she will haunt them, I'm sure.

Bereavement

A lonely figure, plodding on,
No loved one by her side,
No voice to cheer and comfort her,
No arm to hold and guide.
The path is bleak and stony,
The wind is harsh and strong –
You cannot see, but those she loved
Are helping her along.

The Old Tub's Prayer

Don't let me lie on the sand, Lord, beached,
With my timbers cracked and rotting away,
While children play round me most of the day
Crying, "This was a boat, once, this was a boat."

I have struggled like most in the stormy seas,
And the waves have thrown me hither and yon.
I have offered my thanks when the storm has gone,
Crying, "I'm still afloat, Lord, I'm still afloat!"

The rocks have pierced me, you know, O Lord,
And I've longed for the harbour many a day;
But a rest and repaint and I'm up and away,
For I am a boat, Lord, I am a boat.

Let the tide take me out, and I'll take my chance.
I'll ride the storm, or I'll sink like a stone.
Don't let me rot on the beach alone.
I'm still a boat, Lord, I'm still a boat!

The Flower Festival

The church was an old one, gaunt and grey,
And hardly anyone went to pray.
It somehow failed to welcome you in
And made you think of sorrow and sin.

Then somebody said, "We'll fill it with flowers."
The arrangers spent many happy hours
'Til the church was no longer dull and numb.
"Come and rejoice, my people, come."

M. A. P. - OAP

I don't always take my stick,
I don't really need any sympathy,
It's just that I have this dodgy knee.

I don't always take my stick,
Though nowadays I get my kicks
Meeting other people with sticks.

I don't always take my stick,
But it's good for my heart as now I find
People in general are generally kind.

They hold the doors to let me through,
And don't let go as they used to do,
With my stick.

If I should trip on a paving stone,
I could get myself up if I'm all alone
With my stick.

If someone should ever try to attack,
I'd lean on my good leg and give him a whack
With my stick.

Don't despair as the years pass by,
There's a Freedom Pass and stars in the sky,
And a stick.

The Blind Man

"Did you see the sunset ablaze tonight,
Golden and pink in the evening light,
The colours all showing a different hue
Against a sky which was turquoise blue?"
Said the blind man.

"I was catching a train at the end of the day,
With lots of commuters blocking my way.
There wasn't much time to look up at the sky,
So the sunset rather passed me by."

"Did you see the wisteria hanging its head
Over the colourful garden bed,
The lupins standing tall and straight
Down by the little garden gate?"
Said the blind man.

"I'm sure there's a pretty garden view
But I had to take charge of the barbecue.
There's plenty to keep me busy, and then
I can sit in front of the box again."

"Did you see the ducklings crossing the lake,
Leaving a little shimmering wake?
The trees are lovely - you *must* have seen
All those magnificent shades of green?"
Said the blind man.

"I really can't say there was much to see.
A lake's a lake, and a tree's a tree.
And, anyway, the match had begun
So I went in to see if my team had won."

"I'm lucky to have a good memory;
I can conjure up what I want to see.
The pictures are clear enough in my mind -
Do you think perhaps it is you who are blind?"
Said the blind man.

St Giles

Legend has it that St Giles
Inhabited a cave,
And he befriended there a hind
Whose life he sought to save.
The huntsman loosed an arrow
Where he thought the hind to be -
It flew into some bushes
Wounding Giles in the knee.
So patron saint of cripples
And of beggars he was known,
And abbot of a monastery
He founded near the Rhone.
So many centuries have passed,
No building is there still,
But in its place now standing
Is the city of Saint-Gilles.

St Giles the Abbot

On the outskirts of the village
St Giles the Abbot stands,
On what, in Anglo-Saxon times
Were King of Wessex' lands.
Though storm and fire and tempest
Have visited the site,
Through many generations
The candles have burned bright.
So still our feet are treading
Where our English forbears trod
And still St Giles calls us
To the worshipping of God.
And now the church is standing
With buttresses and friends,
To keep it in position
'Til the next millennium ends.

Mrs McCarthy

You can't help liking Mrs McCarthy.
She stirs up trouble wherever she goes;
She doesn't like dirt, and she can't stand rudeness;
She can't abide people in 'don't care' clothes.
She hates to see anyone drinking, and chewing,
Out in the streets as they lazily roam -
It's normal for cattle and sheep, but people?
Can't they wait 'til they get back home?
You can't help cheering Mrs McCarthy.
She loathes a liar, or scrounger, or cheat;
She has only contempt for the gravy-trainers
Who like to fatten on other folk's meat.
She has a good heart, has Mrs McCarthy;
There's no doubt at all she's the salt of the earth.
If she thinks that something is wrong, or dishonest,
She'll fight against it for all she's worth.
She cares for manners does Mrs McCarthy -
Not always taught in the home or school.
She thinks of others in all her dealings
And tries to live by the golden rule.
Onward, onward, Mrs McCarthy,
March as a Christian on to war.
You may not win, but we're right behind you -
All of us know what you're fighting for.

The Convalescent Home

I lay in the convalescent home
Clinging to life and hope,
And prayed as the waves crashed over me
That someone would throw me a rope.

I pressed the bell and an angel came in
And flooded the room with light;
She was dressed as a nurse - I could see the blue -
But I knew what she was all right.

"You know," she said, as she tended me
And gave me her gentle care,
"I think all you patients are wonderful
With the things you have to bear."

"Oh no, it is *you* who are wonderful.
God bless all you nurses," I said.
"Though the doctors have saved me, I needed your help
To rise again from my bed."

Spring

You gave me, Lord, another spring,
To hear at dawn the chorus sing,
And see the snowdrop's gentle head
Light up the winter sleeping bed.
The crocus - golden, mauve and white -
The tulips and the aconite,
The daffodils, with golden blaze
Illuminating garden ways,
The almond pink, the cherry too,
Camellias of blushing hue.
I have so loved to see it all,
But now the blossoms start to fall
And all the early glory's done.
Please grant me, Lord, another one -
Another lovely English spring,
Another rich awakening.

Father Knows Best

"Don't do it," he said. "You'll regret it.
You'll be sorry you didn't think twice."
But I did, and I do, and I am, so
Next time I shall heed his advice.

Thoughts of a Senior Citizen

I tidied my pantry this morning;
I do it whenever I'm free.
I check over all 'best before' dates,
Now everything's as it should be.
It was rather a shock to discover
Baked beans may last longer than me!

Words from Chambers Dictionary

(to which I am beholden)

I came across the word bethump
When looking under B.
Then found I could bethink betimes
Bewildered though I be.
And woe betide if you're bethwacked!
It would betoss your head,
Though if you are betoiled you can
Betake you to your bed.
My mind is now betumbled, so,
Betwixt yourself and me,
I think it does behove me to
Betake myself to C.

McTavish

McTavish was growing older
And felt he should turn to prayer,
So he went to a building marked 'Free Church'
As there'd be no collection there.

The Skies

Do not neglect to raise your eyes
To watch the glory of the skies.
It's always there for us to see,
Provided absolutely free.
We cannot guess how much it's worth
To view the greatest show on earth.

England

I love the fields of England
That are not built on yet.
Oh, feast your eyes upon them so
You never can forget
That where the ugly buildings stand,
And where the road is wide,
Was once a glorious heritage
Of English countryside.
Think shame that there were those who
Didn't seem to care at all,
That men who farmed for England had
Their backs against the wall.
They didn't ask for sympathy,
A pat upon the head,
But wanted what they all deserved:
The chance to earn their bread –
The chance to farm the English fields,
To plough and sow and reap,
To tend their flocks as always.
God, how can the English sleep?
Wake! Save the green of England.
The clock of progress ticks,
So act before developers
Have covered it with bricks.

Christmas

Christmas is coming! Oh, not again!
The drunks who never know when to say when;
The table laden with many a treat,
Far more food than we'll ever eat;
The human hippos, with greedy eyes,
Gobbling up turkey and pudding and pies;
The battling housewife, held in a queue,
Using her elbows to help her through.

"Do you know, do you know what it's all about?"
"Oh, go and get lost while we bellow and shout!"

Everyone knows it is really great
To have good reason to celebrate,
To remember the birth of Mary's son,
But not when it's horribly overdone.
Why not let all the excesses be
In thankfulness, thoughtfulness, jollity?
Perhaps this Christmas I'll do my part
By letting my actions be all from my heart.
God bless you, neighbours, from me and mine,
And may I ask you to pass the wine?

At Your Service

Thank you for calling this number.
We're here to be helpful to you,
And if that is what you have rung for,
Perhaps you would kindly press 2.
You now have a number of options,
Which we're sure you'll agree makes it fun.
If you want to give vent to your feelings,
Then may we suggest you press 1.
If you've had no reply to your letter
And you feel it is long overdue,
Though they may have gone off for a coffee
You could just take a chance and press 2.
If you're quite satisfied with our service
And you'd like to advise us, feel free.
This line isn't used very often
But why not just try it - press 3.
If you're feeling bewildered already
We can soon cheer you up, we are sure,
For - surprise! - there are real live people
You can speak to - so go on, press 4.
We're sorry you've got the engaged tone,
Our staff are aware of your call,
And as they are all very busy
We will play you the Dead March in *Saul*.

Nil Desperandum!

I love my little garden
And watch it while it grows -
The apple blossom coming out,
The tulips and the rose.
It should be very peaceful,
A place to meditate,
But now I've bought a book which tells
Me of my garden's fate.
There are several sorts of beetle
That might come to visit me,
And something that is listed as
A small leafcutter bee.
While I admire the blossoms
In an outlook that is fair,
I can't see the mites and weevils
And the bugs that flourish there.
I look for powdery mildew,
For aphis and for rust.
Of course the slugs and snails will turn
Your garden dreams to dust.
Though it is bright and beautiful,
The creatures that are small,
If you'll forgive my saying so,
Don't seem much good at all.

NHS

The patient lying near to me
Just cannot eat the food.
She thinks the ward is crowded
And the nursing staff are rude.
When *she* calls for attention
No one answers at a run.
She's rather near the window
And she doesn't like the sun.
Her bed must not be moved because
It might go near the door.
A draught would make her stiff,
And now her bottom's getting sore.
The patient on her right
Is too exuberant by half;
The one who's on her left
Can never seem to raise a laugh.
She thinks a germ attacked her
While on holiday in Rome.
They'll never really cure her
So she might as well go home.

The Pearly Gates

Three times I've neared the Pearly Gates.
Alas, I'm only mortal!
But so far I've not been allowed
Within the heavenly portal.

No doubt the guardian of the gates
One day will be relenting,
But meanwhile I'm enjoying life
And doing some repenting.

Love Letters

I kept your letters through the years
Tied in a ribbon band,
So always I can read again
The words in your dear hand.

I know I never shall forget
Who all those notes were from.
They touch my heart much more than any
Dot dot slash dot com.

Road Rage

The motorist behind me
Is really rather dim;
And if he wasn't quite so big,
I'd have some words with him.
He doesn't seem to notice
What to me is clear:
That if I step upon the brake
He'll hit me in the rear.
If some endangered species
Should want to cross the road,
Which one should I attempt to save,
The roadhog or a toad?
I'm driving on the highway
According to the law –
Well, actually, I see that I
Am doing thirty-four.
I try to be a Christian
And think of other folk,
It may be he has heard his home
Is going up in smoke.
Perhaps his dear old mother
Has lost the front door key,
And he is rushing to her aid
As quickly as can be.
At last he's overtaken
And disappeared in dust.
He will not meet an obstacle
Around the bend, I trust.
I think as he was passing
He turned and waved his hand,
Unless it was a gesture
That I didn't understand.

The Queen's English

One thing I do not like to see
Is a wrongly placed apostrophe.
It is a mystery to me
To find it where it should not be.

John has a book so it is John's book,
The cook's hat shows it belongs to Cook.
It would be simple if one took
The time to have a second look.

If you sell apples, beans and peas,
Or maybe offer afternoon teas,
Or want to advertise your fees,
They need no apostrophe, if you please.

* * * * *

Our friends invited Johnny and me
To join them for a cup of tea.
It's not too hard to reason why
They would not invite Johnny and I.
The simple rule will always be
If there were no Johnny they would invite me.

Of course if we wanted to ask *them* to tea
Johnny and *I* would invite them - you see?

Medical History

I suppose there is an 'itis'
That I haven't suffered from,
Though I have had far more
Than any Harry, Dick or Tom.
It's difficult to spell them,
Sometimes leaving me perplexed.
By the time I've learned to spell one
I am starting on the next.
I always see the doctor but
When knocking on his door
I know I've got an 'itis'
That I haven't had before.
He never loses patience
And I know he won't complain,
Even though I'm sure he's thinking
'Oh, she can't be back AGAIN!'

Strained Relations

Take out his meal from the micro, Mother,
You won't hear his key in the door,
He's stuck on the M25, dear,
And he may be a day or two more.

His slippers can leave his armchair, Mother,
He's standing jam-packed in a train.
By the time he has taken his shoes off,
They'll have to go back on again.

Don't fret if he doesn't turn up, dear,
It's not because he doesn't care;
He's caught between four sets of roadworks
And enjoying the scenery there.

Don't wait for him, dear, at the airport,
He's still overseas on the ground.
He loves you, dear Mother; however,
A mechanical fault has been found.

Don't let it upset you, dear Mother;
He wanted to heal the rift,
But he's caught on the 24th floor, dear,
As something's gone wrong with the lift.